Yī Ér Sān

MY FIRST CHINESE RHYMES

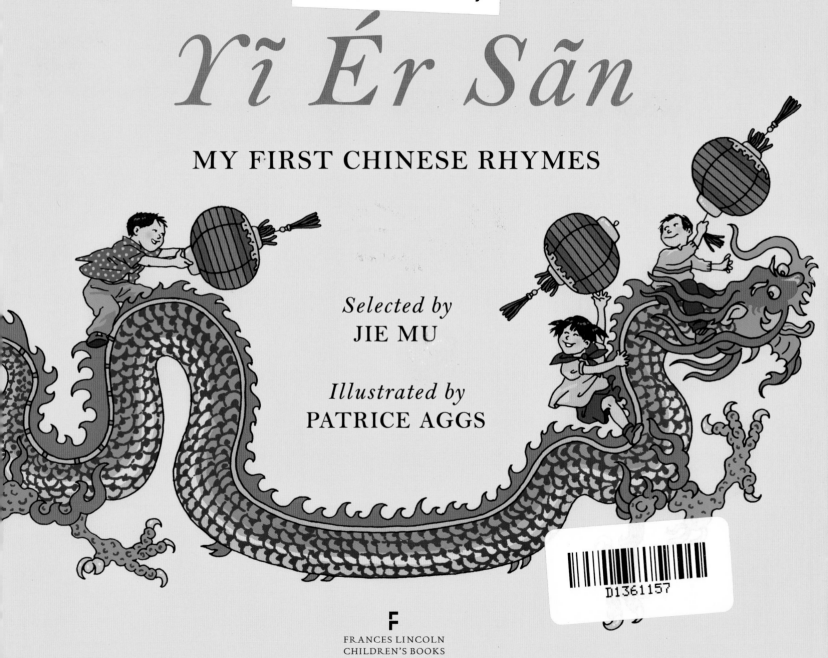

Selected by
JIE MU

Illustrated by
PATRICE AGGS

F

FRANCES LINCOLN
CHILDREN'S BOOKS

Contents

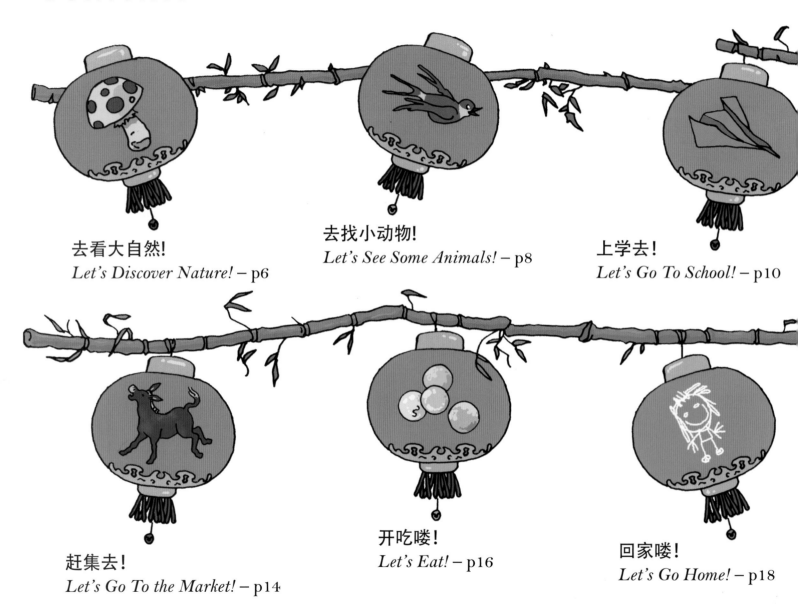

Yī Ér Sān

The rhymes I have selected for this book have been handed down through the generations in China. Not only can they be used as a stepping-stone for learning Mandarin Chinese, but these rhymes and songs also take us on a journey through Chinese culture.

We start by visiting nature, which is a vital part of Chinese children's lives. Adults often encourage children to engage with nature because it is a fundamental part of life. Well-balanced people are in-tune with nature. We also find several family themes in the book. Family bonds play an important role in Chinese society and there are many songs and rhymes about these special relationships.

In many rhymes and songs, we explore moral values. These morals stem from Confucianism – a cornerstone of Chinese culture that has lasted for over 2,000 years. Children are taught to behave properly ("Find a penny"), study hard ("A little schoolboy") and have good manners ("Sit and wait").

The guide at the back of the book explains the rhymes as well as some cultural elements. Useful phrases are highlighted for children to use in simple conversations. To help children with their pronunciation and to learn the songs and rhymes, there is an audio CD.

 Look for the yellow dots to learn new words.

Join me on a journey through Chinese songs and rhymes, and let's have some fun!

玩儿去!
Let's Play! – p12

睡觉觉!
Let's Go To Sleep! – p20

去看大自然!

让我们荡起双桨,

小船儿推开波浪。

海面倒映着美丽的白塔,

四周环绕着绿树红墙。

小船儿轻轻,

飘荡在水中,

迎面吹来了凉爽的风。

葡萄

船

阿门阿前一棵葡萄树，

阿嫩阿嫩绿地刚发芽，

蜗牛背着那重重的壳呀，

一步一步地往上爬。

阿树阿上两只黄鹂鸟，

阿嘻阿嘻哈哈在笑它，

葡萄成熟还早得很哪，

现在你上来干什么？

阿黄阿黄鹂儿不要笑，

等我爬上它就成熟了。

蘑菇

采蘑菇的小姑娘，

背着一个大竹筐，

清晨光着小脚丫，

走遍森林和山冈。

她采的蘑菇最多，

多得像那星星数不清。

她采的蘑菇最大，

大得像那小伞装满筐。

去找小动物！

小兔子乖乖，

把门儿开开，

快点儿开开，

我要进来。

不开、不开、我不开，

妈妈没回来，

谁来也不开。

小兔子乖乖，

把门儿开开，

快点儿开开，

我要进来。

就开、就开、我就开，

妈妈回来了，

快点把门开。

鸟

树

石头

山

小燕子，穿花衣，
年年春天来这里。
我问燕子你为啥来，
燕子说，这里的春天最美丽。

两只老虎，两只老虎，
跑得快，跑得快。
一只没有眼睛，
一只没有尾巴，
真奇怪，真奇怪！

虫虫飞，虫虫飞，
飞到南山吃露水
露水吃不到，回来吃青草。

上学去！

小嘛小儿郎，

背着那书包上学堂，

不怕太阳晒，

也不怕那风雨狂，

只怕先生骂我懒哪，

没有学问啰无脸见爹娘，

朗里格朗里呀朗格里格朗，

没有学问啰无脸见爹娘。

纸飞机

你拍一，我拍一，
一个小孩坐飞机。
你拍二，我拍二，
两个小孩梳小辫儿。
你拍三，我拍三，
三个小孩吃饼干。
你拍四，我拍四，
四个小孩写大字。

一二三四五，
上山打老虎。
老虎打不到，
打到小松鼠。
松鼠有几只，
让我数一数。
数去又数来，
一二三四五。

玩儿去！

丢手绢，丢手绢，

轻轻地放在小朋友的后面，

大家不要告诉他。

快点快点抓住他，快点快点抓住他。

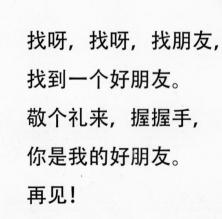

找呀，找呀，找朋友，

找到一个好朋友。

敬个礼来，握握手，

你是我的好朋友。

再见！

滑板车

一个毽子踢三踢，

马兰花开二十一。

二五六，二五七，

二八、二九、三十一，

三五六，三五七，

三八、三九、四十一，

……

花园

运动鞋

赶集去！

我在马路边捡到一分钱，
把它交到警察叔叔手里面，
叔叔拿着钱，对我把头点，
我高兴地说了声叔叔再见。

自行车

篮子

三轮车，跑得快，
上面坐个老太太，
要五毛，给一块，
你说奇怪不奇怪。

驴

帽子

泥

车轮

我有一只小毛驴，我从来也不骑。
有一天我心血来潮，骑着去赶集。
我手里拿着小皮鞭，我心里正得意。
不知怎么哗拉拉拉，我摔了一身泥。

开吃喽！

卖汤圆，卖汤圆，

小二哥的汤圆是圆又圆。

一碗汤圆满又满，三毛钱呀买一碗。

汤圆汤圆卖汤圆，汤圆一样可以当茶饭，

唉嗨哟........

汤圆汤圆卖汤圆，汤圆一样可以当茶饭。

排排坐，

吃果果。

你一个，我一个，

妹妹睡着了，给她留一个，

给她留一个呀。

婴儿车

毯子

月亮

桥

八月十五月儿明呀，
爷爷为我打月饼呀。
月饼圆圆甜又香啊，
一块月饼一片情啊。

摇，摇，摇，
摇到外婆桥。
外婆叫我好宝宝，
糖一包，果一包，
又有团子又有糕。

回家喽！

爸爸

妈妈

我的家庭真可爱，
整洁美满又安康。
姐妹兄弟很和气，
父母都慈祥。
虽然没有好花园，
春兰秋桂长飘香。
虽然没有大厅堂，
冬天温暖夏天凉。
可爱的家庭呀，
我不能离开你，
你的恩惠比天长。

世上只有妈妈好，

有妈的孩子像个宝，

投进了妈妈的怀抱，幸福享不了。

世上只有妈妈好，

没妈的孩子像根草，

离开妈妈的怀抱，幸福哪里找？

我画爸爸，妈妈笑。

我画妈妈，爸爸笑。

我画我呀，

爸爸妈妈一起笑。

猫

跳绳

画笔

睡觉觉！

睡吧，睡吧，
我亲爱的宝贝，
妈妈的双手轻轻摇着你。
摇篮摇你，快快安睡。
夜已安静，被里多温暖。

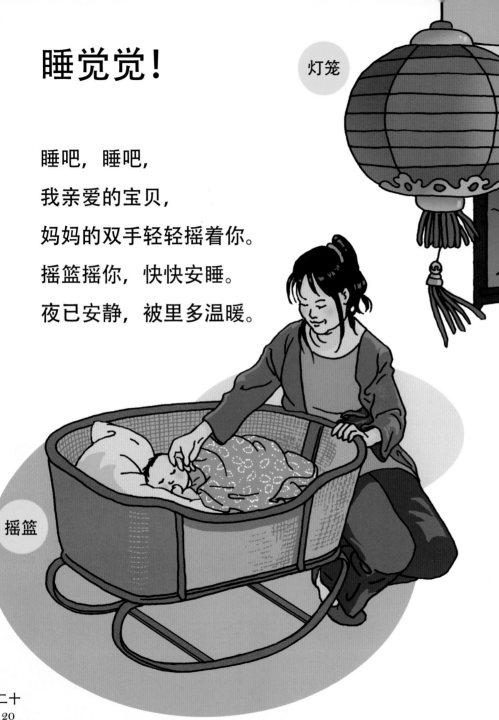

灯笼

窗

摇篮

月儿明，风儿静，
树叶儿遮窗棂 啊。
蛐蛐儿叫铮铮，
好比那琴弦声 啊。
琴声儿轻，调儿动听，
摇篮轻摆动啊。
娘的宝宝，闭上眼睛，
睡了那个，睡在梦中。

蓝蓝的天空银河里，

有只小白船，

船上有棵桂花树，

白兔在游玩。

桨儿桨儿看不见，船上也没帆，

飘呀飘呀飘向西天。

床

去看大自然！– Let's discover nature!

Useful phrases:
让我们：Let us
等我：When I, as I

让我们荡起双桨 - Let's row our boat

A group of children row a boat and have fun outdoors.
Let us row our paddles, | The boat pushes through the waves. | On the surface of the lake reflects the beautiful white tower, | Surrounded by green trees and red walls. | The little boat is floating gently on the water, | A cool wind is blowing to our faces.

蜗牛和黄鹂鸟 - A snail and yellowbirds

This funny rhyme is a short conversation between two yellowbirds and a snail, who is slowly climbing up a tree. The story is about perseverance and early preparation. In the first two lines, the word 啊 (a) (repeated four times) is nonsense but it's fun to say.

采蘑菇的小姑娘 - A mushroom-picking girl

A happy song about a little girl who picks mushrooms in the country.

去找小动物！– Let's see some animals!

Useful phrases:
乖乖：good boy
我要进来：let me in
我不：I will not

小兔子乖乖 – Little baby rabbit

One of the first rhymes for many Chinese children. It tells a story of a baby rabbit who is left at home by his mum. Later, a wolf knocks on the door, disguised as mother rabbit. But the baby rabbit is very clever and does not fall for the wolf's tricks. "Guai guai" often means a clever child or a good boy.

小燕子 - Little swallow

This rhyme was written in the 1950s when factories were being built in China. The people hoped that wildlife like the swallow would still visit areas with new, big buildings in the spring.

虫虫飞 - Bug, bug fly

A rhyme that invites children to get close to nature and notice even the smallest things around them.

两只老虎 - Two tigers

Children love to recite this popular Chinese nursery rhyme.
Two tigers, two tigers, | Running fast, running fast. | One of them has no eyes, | One of them has no tail, | Very strange, very strange! |

上学去！– Let's go to school!

Useful phrases:
梳小辫儿：braid hair
写大字：write characters

读书郎 - A little schoolboy

This lively song encourages children to study hard at 学校 (school).

你拍一，我拍一 - You make one, I make one

A fun counting rhyme in which children learn how to share.
You make one, I make one. | One child takes a plane. | You make two, I make two. | Two children braid their hair. | You make three, I make three. | Three children eat biscuits. | You make four, I make four. | Four children write characters.

五指歌 - Five-finger counting

Children learn to use their fingers to help them count in this fun rhyme, which is also a short hunting story.

玩儿去！– Let's play!

Useful phrases:
握手：shake hand
快点：quick
再见：goodbye

丢手绢 - Drop handkerchief

This rhyme is used to play a game similar to "duck, duck, goose". One child in the circle is the "dropper". The "dropper" walks outside the circle, drops the handkerchief behind another player and starts to run. The child with the handkerchief dropped to his or her back must run around the circle to catch the "dropper".

找朋友 - Seek a pal

Pairs of children dance together in this fun rhyme, which is repeated as many times as needed. Each time the rhyme ends, the children change partners and seek a new pal. The rhyme teaches that it is easier for you to make friends when you are polite and kind.
Seek, seek, seek a pal, | I have found a best pal. | Shake hands and bow, | You are my best friend now. | Goodbye!

跳皮筋 - Rubber band skipping

A very popular game among Chinese girls. While skipping, the girls recite this counting rhyme.
Kick a shuttlecock three times, | Flowers are blooming, twenty-one. | Twenty-five, six, twenty-five, seven, | Twenty-eight, twenty-nine, thirty-one, | Thirty-five, six, thirty-five, seven, | Thirty-eight, thirty-nine, forty-one . . .